LION
CHAMELEON
CAMEL
RAVEN
MOUSE
SEAGULLS
CORGI DOG
BUTTERFLY
BULL
ZEBRA
HEDGEHOGS
TIGER

SEAL
COCKATOO
MARINE ANGELFISH
MEERKATS
BEETLE
PANTHER
TURTLE
SNAKE
CROWNED CRANE BIRDS
DEER
OSTRICH
RACCOONS
BEAR

The «One Color Relaxation» book series is the most stress-free coloring you'd ever tried! No thoughts. No extra skills. So fun and easy to color!

Color the attractive magic LINES with just ONE COLOR of pen, pencil or marker to get 25 amazing pictures with animals. For better results use dark colors.

Listen to the radio, your favorite music or audio-book and enjoy your internal harmony while coloring.

This is the perfect book to take on the go as it is of the letter-size format and lightweight.

Relax just with ONE COLOR!

mail@sunlifedrawing.com
www.sunlifedrawing.com

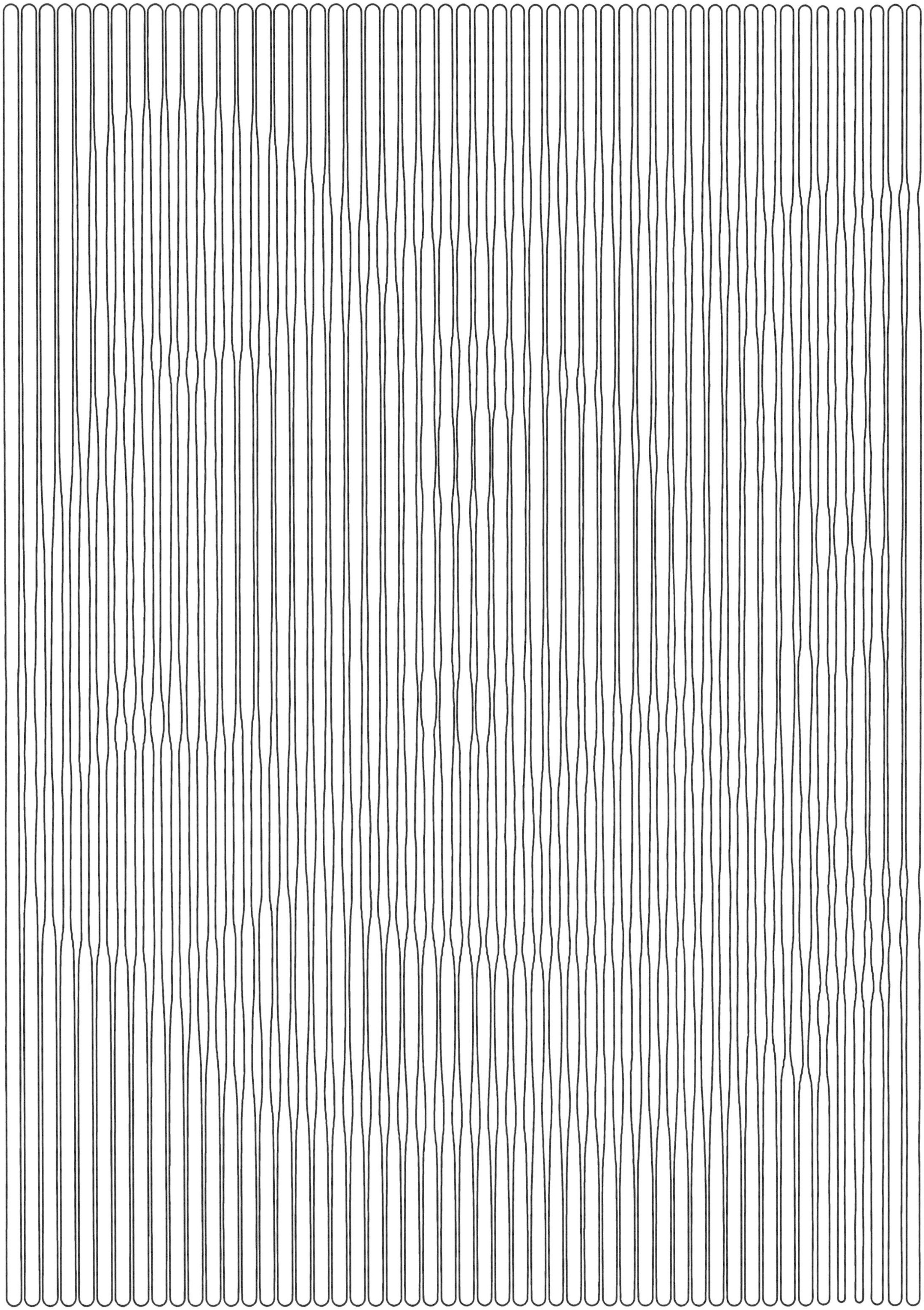

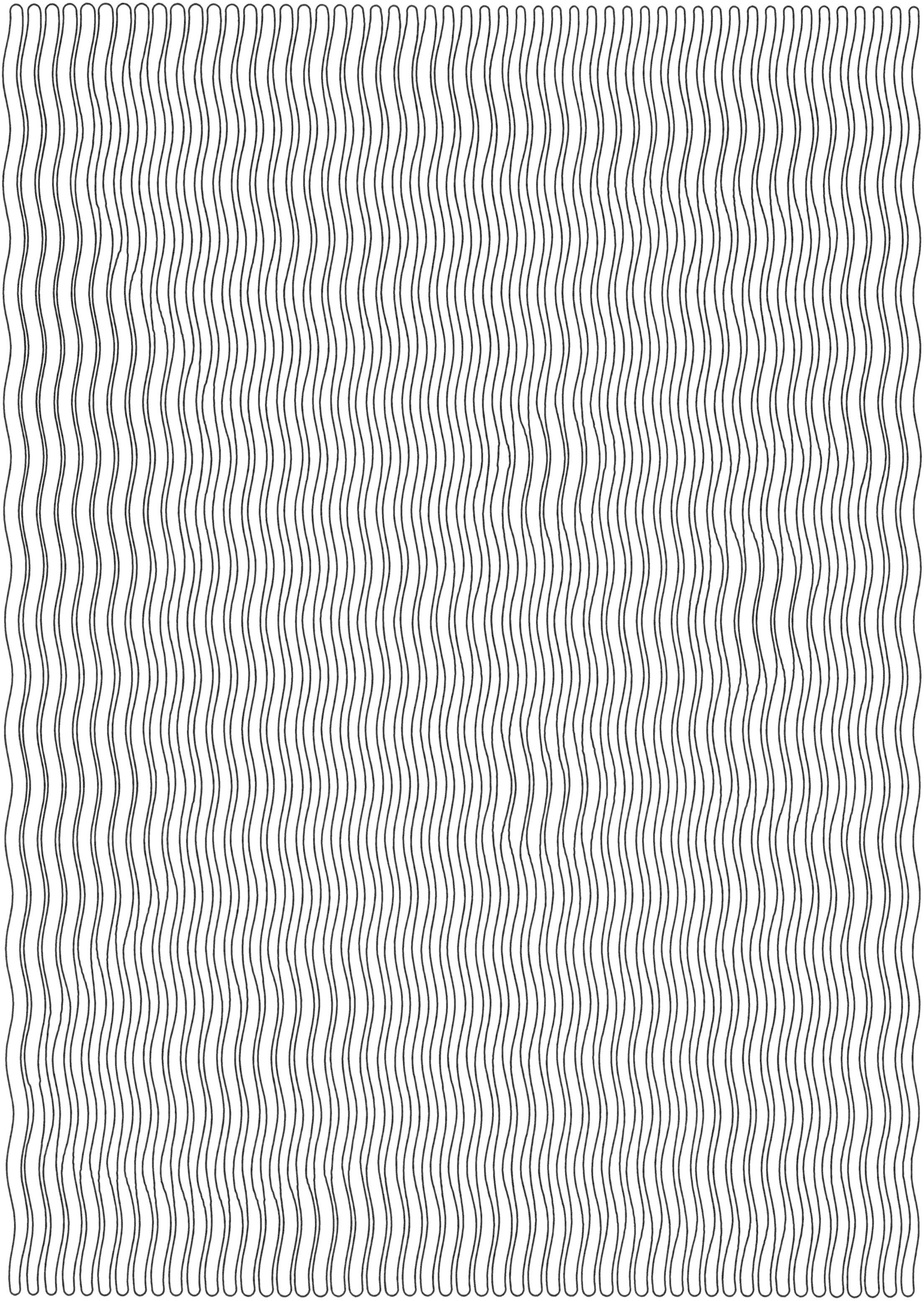

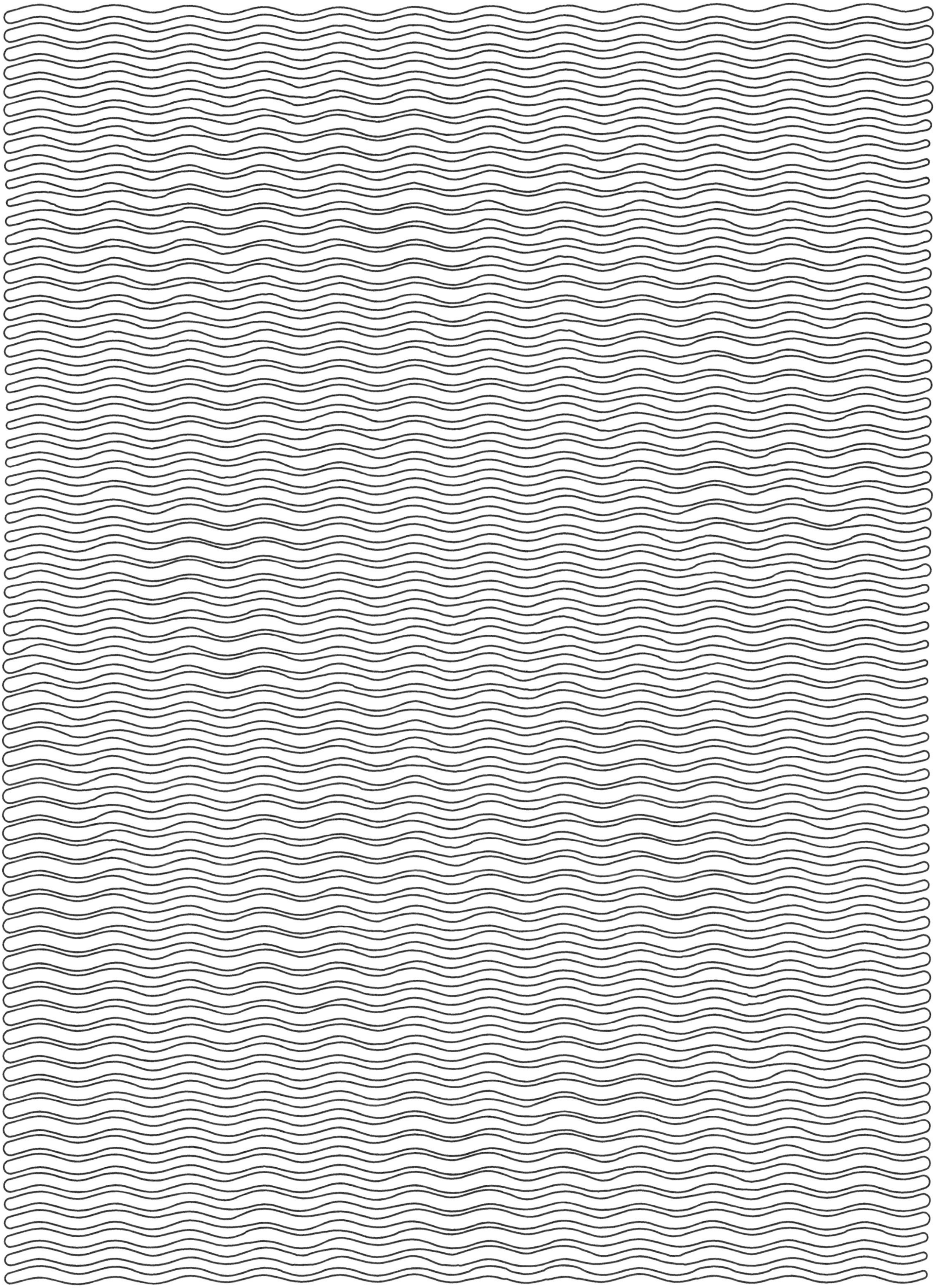

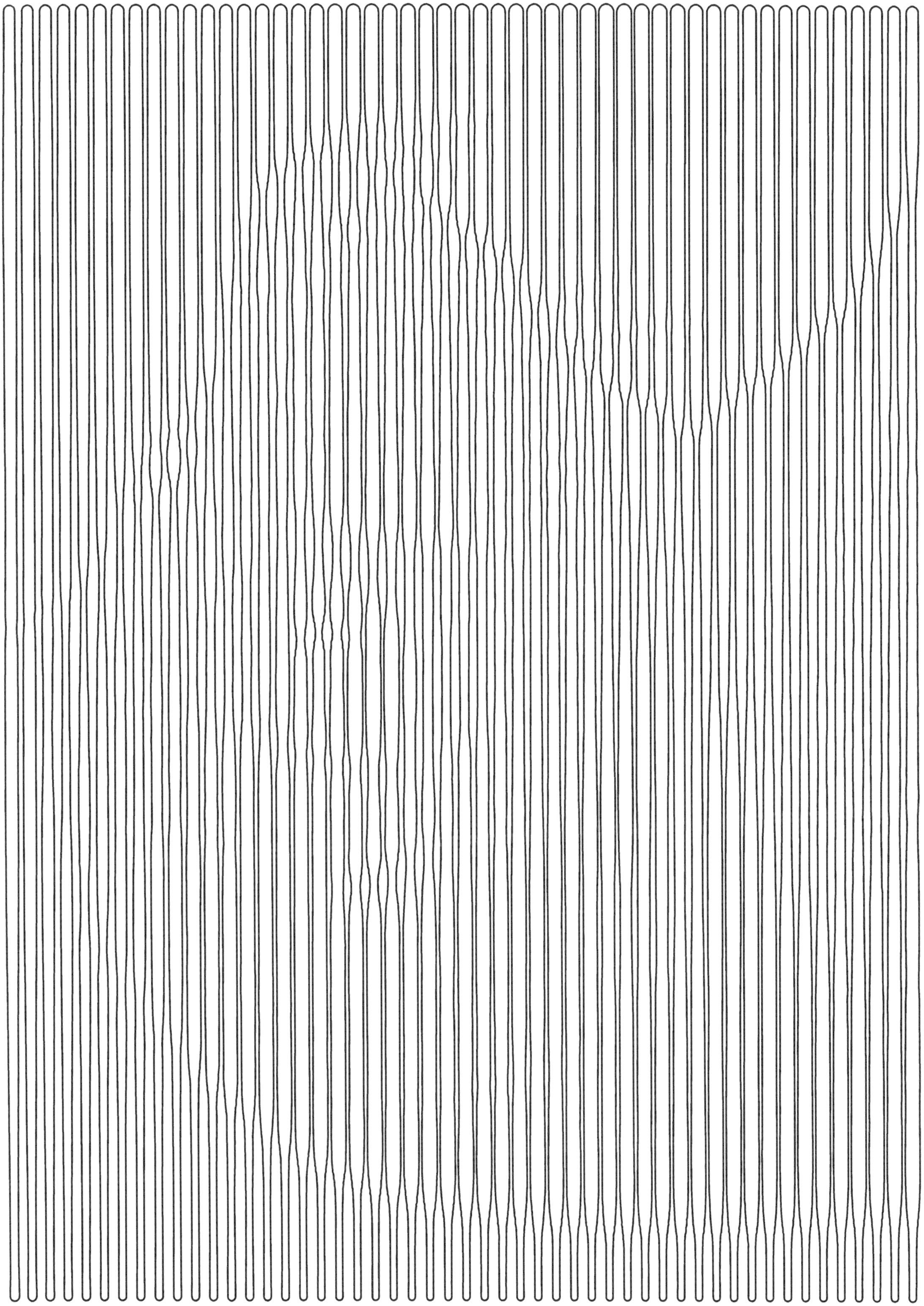

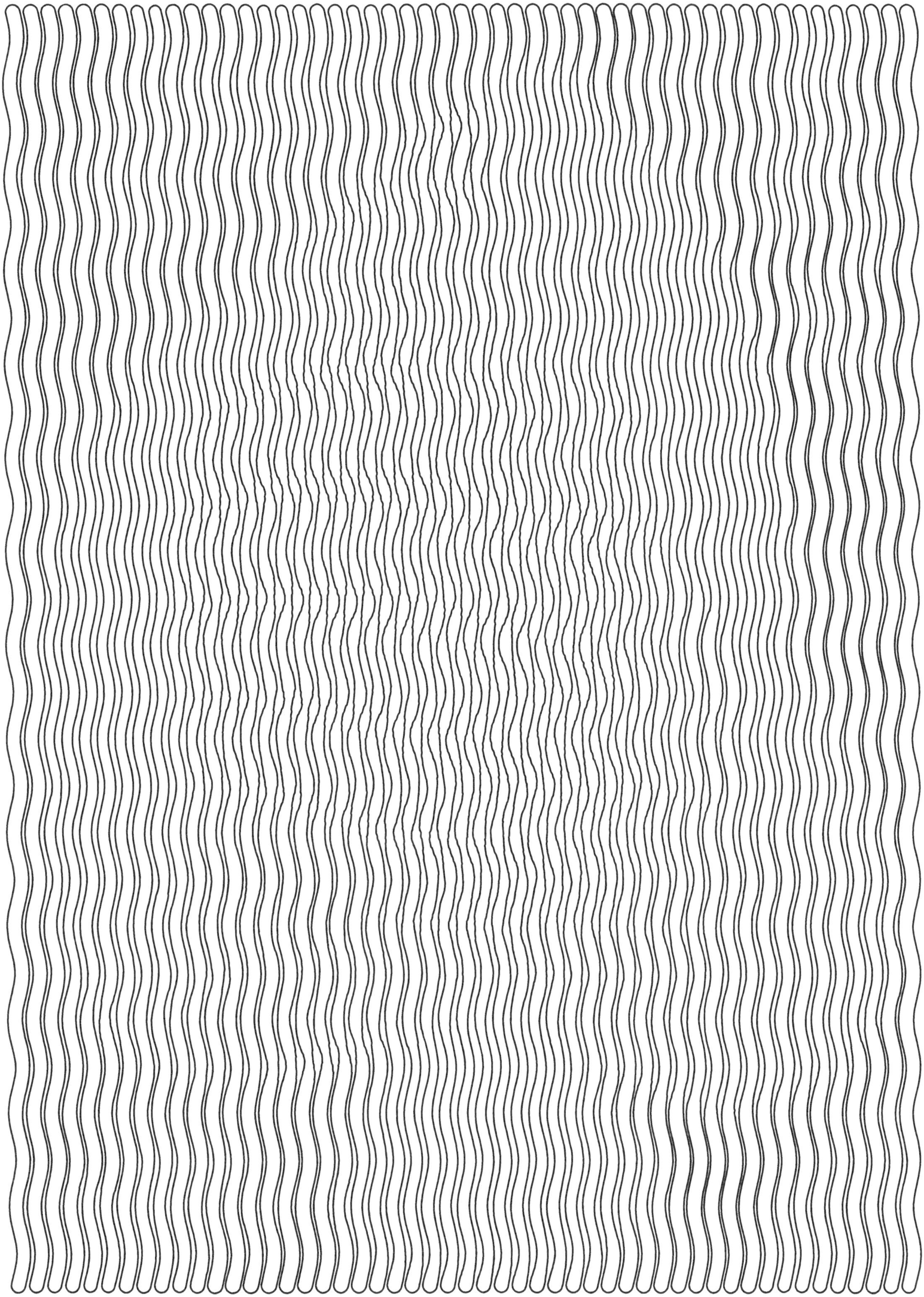

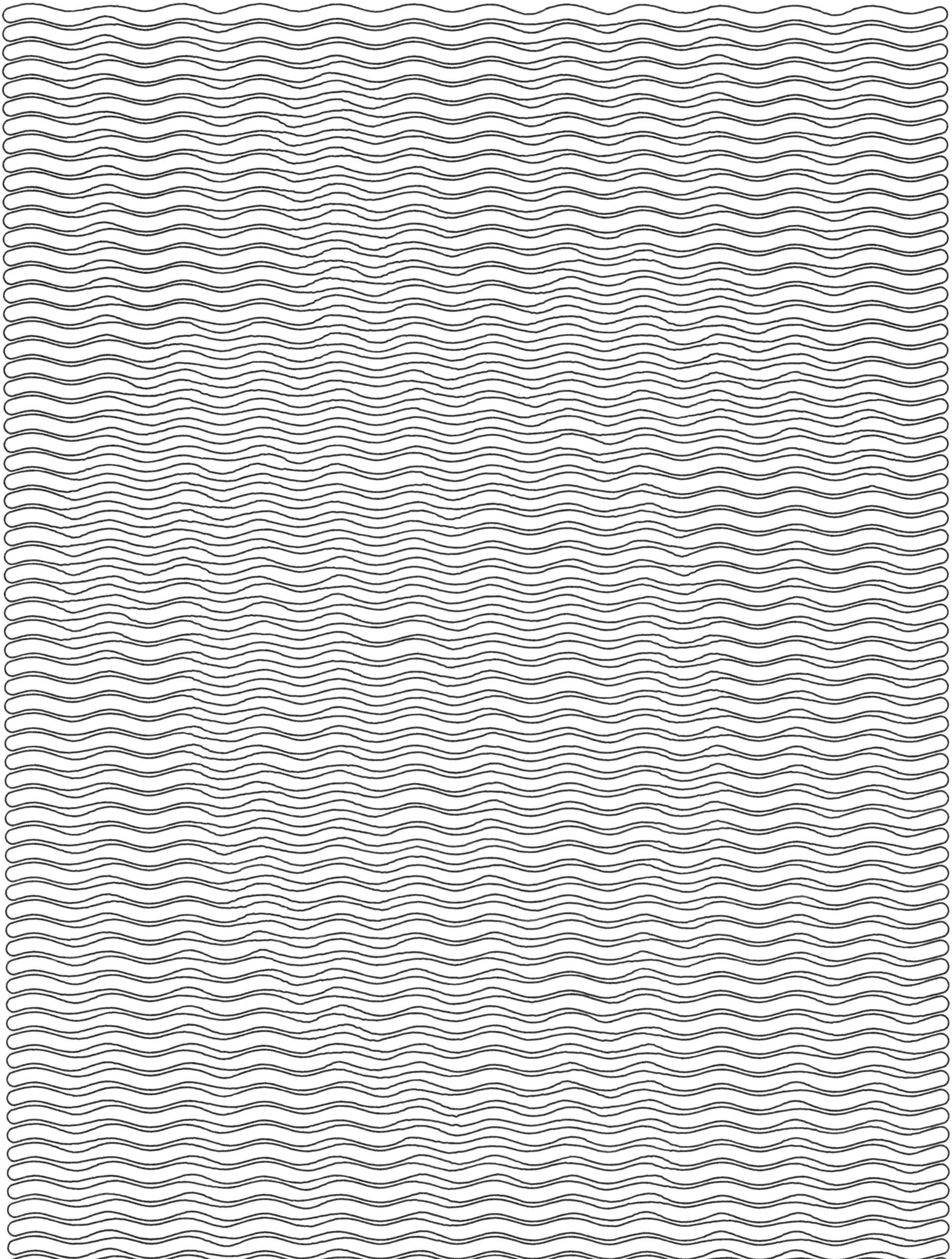

THANK YOU

for choosing this book! If you enjoyed it, please write YOUR REVIEW on Amazon. We love hearing from our customers and your opinion is very important for us to make our books better.

FOLLOW US

Twitter.com/SunlifeDrawing

Facebook.com/SunlifeDrawing

Instagram.com/SunlifeDrawing

Trial Page from the book «One Color DOTS: Animals»

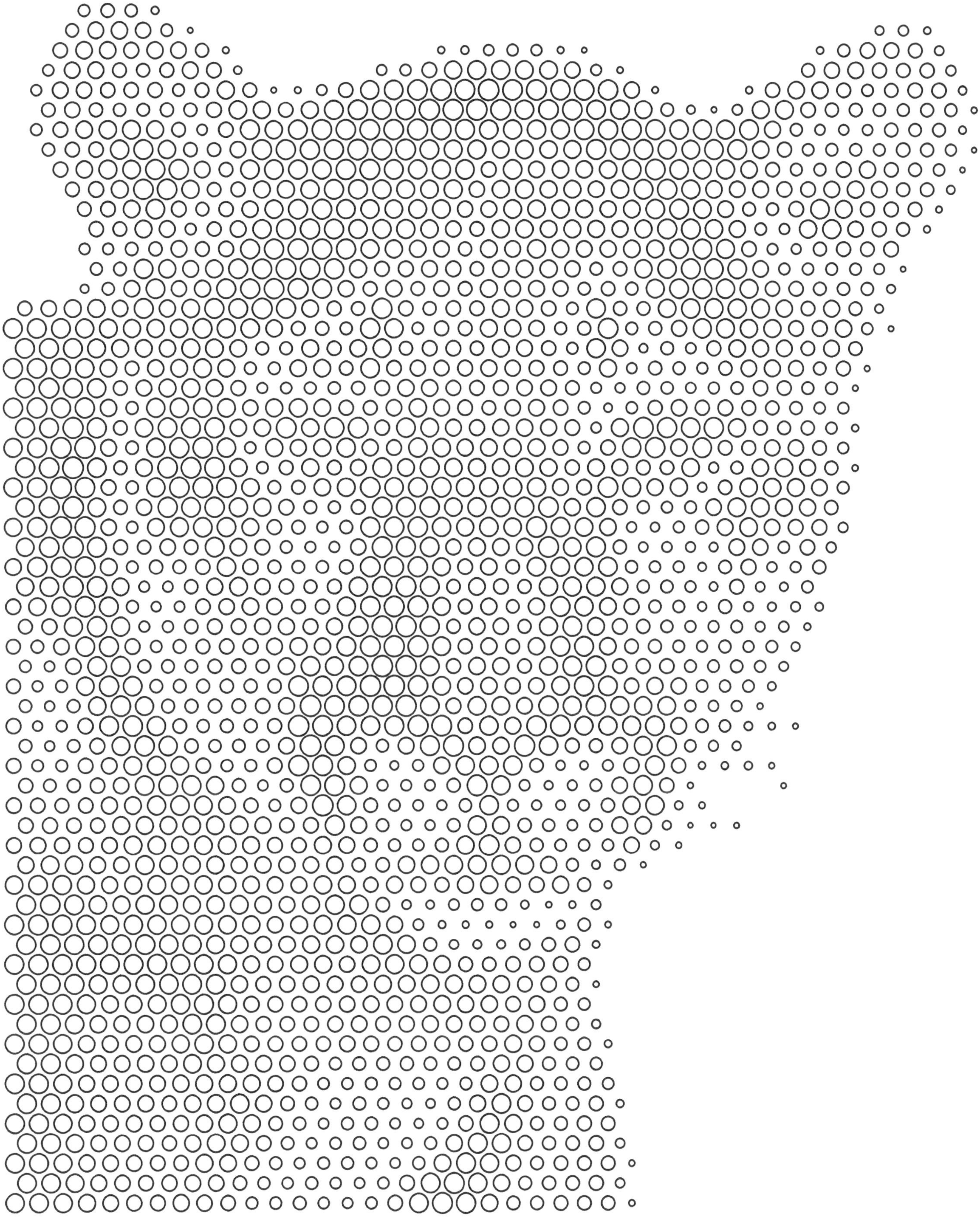

www.ingramcontent.com/pod-product-compliance
Lightning Source LLC
Chambersburg PA
CBHW062342220526
45469CB00008B/2805
* 9 7 8 1 7 2 5 0 8 2 4 2 7 *